WHAT THE HECK IS FOREX

Six Simple Steps to Profit Trading Currencies in the Foreign Exchange Market

Dr Gregory Arana

Table of Contents

INTRODUCTION 1

WHAT IS THAT IN THE SKY? IS IT A BIRD? A PLANE? NO IT IS A FOREX TRADER? 3

WHAT ARE THE 6 SECRET STEPS to go from zero to hero in the Forex market?? 6

Chapter 1 7

Chapter 2 21

    WHAT THE HECK IS FOREX? 21

    CAESAR 23

Chapter 3 27

    HOW DOES THE FOREX MARKET MOVE? 27

    Measuring Currency Strength and Weakness 31

Chapter 4 35

    WHAT ARE THE FOREX BASICS?? WHAT ARE THE BREAD AND BUTTER OF CURRENCY TRADING? 35

Chapter 5 40

    SUPPORT AND RESISTANCE 40

    SUPPORT is a FLOOR 41

    RESISTANCE is a CEILING 41

    Which Forex mentor is right for you? 45

Summary of Forex trading method and your opportunity 50

    BEFORE SELL ORDER 51

    AFTER SELL ORDER 52

Disclaimer: Foreign currency exchange is a difficult concept to explain and trading this market is tough to profit from consistently. There is a risk of losing some or all your initial investment.

INTRODUCTION

There are hundreds of books and blogs about the forex market. What makes this book special??

I have a special ability to take complex concepts and make them simple to understand. This book introduces you to what the basics of forex are.

It also takes you on a quick journey from not knowing **wtf** forex is about .. to trading a demo account with a forex broker .

I have invested thousands of dollars in learning about this market. Thousands of teachers and forex mentors exist , using many combinations of methods of trading and investing.

It is easy to get overwhelmed and swamped with information overload.

I am here to introduce you to C.A.E.S.E.R.

This is a mnemonic I created to make sense out of all the Forex noise and distraction and get you on the road to practice and profit rapidly.

Let me be clear. This is a complex market and there is a lot to learn. What I have provided in this book is a basic starter kit.

At the end of reading this book you will know enough about the opportunity in this market to make a decision.

You will decide to practice and learn to trade for a full time independent income.

Forex trading is not a hobby.

If you want to lose money…the casino is a much more enjoyable way to go. There are usually free drinks and food for gamblers.

We are in a time of rapid development and expansion of technology and financial markets. There is a need for balance in your investments.

I would suggest that you explore Forex investing as one source of income that has the potential to grow to greatness, if done well.

WTF book is here to help you look back in a year or two and say with conviction: WTF? I am a millionaire!!

If this book makes you a hundredaire or thousandaire?? Would my blueprint be worth it?? The appropriate answer is yes and yes.

WHAT IS THAT IN THE SKY? IS IT A BIRD? A PLANE? NO IT IS A FOREX TRADER?

I know you may be wondering what on earth could a bird's eye view have to do with trading Forex???.

I was traveling to Maryland a few weeks ago to attend a training with master marketer Anik Singal .

My mentor's group of companies grossed $50 million in revenue online last year. I like to invest with and learn from the best.

I was gazing out the plane's window daydreaming about what it steps to take to become a millionaire.

We were cruising high in the sky and I was gazing down at a fluffy blanket of white clouds.

As the plane started to descend for landing, I kept thinking that this is how a bird, a plane or even Superman must feel .

Flying through the air faster than a speeding bullet!

At first, the ground was far away, and you could not see any patterns clearly.

As the plane got lower and lower you first saw the outline of the houses, and then major highways come into view.

The lower the plane got to the airport, the clearer everything became.

The madness of DC area rush hour traffic on the beltway popped into view.

You could see hundreds of cars moving in different directions as the smaller, narrower roads and houses became visible.

(Cars going north are the buyers and cars going south are the sellers...Details in your free report at www.firedupforex.com*)*

Just before touching down for landing, my view narrowed dramatically.

Only the airport runway was visible outside the plane window. (this is a scalper's view of the forex market)

I had an aha moment!! Read about my breakthrough and why the ***market is a snake*** at www.firedupforex.com

A forex trader gets profit by recognizing patterns. If you are trading the GBP/USD (Great British Pound/US dollar) for example; you may be able to see a bearish (selling) pattern on the weekly chart.

You descend a little to the daily chart view to analyze and check if there is a pattern there to buy or sell.

Lastly, you look at the hourly chart to determine what that pattern is and what is the current market direction,

Question : Should I enter the market buying? or selling?.

Question: Is the market so choppy today that I should stay out and protect my profits until tomorrow??

The patterns become clearer as you zoom in . This simple analysis strategy greatly increases your chance for consistent success.

If you would like to descend into a deeper understanding of the mysteries of landing success in your forex trading, visit www.firedupforex.com and get a free copy of ***"the FX market is a snake".***

You are not a bird., you are not a plane. you are not even Superman!!!!.

But I can show you how to become a superb Forex trader!!

I promise you will be entertained and educated at www.firedupforex.com

WHAT ARE THE 6 SECRET STEPS to go from zero to hero in the Forex market??

1. CAESER ...conquer your fears, awaken your inner greatness and become a Forex Emperor

C is for CURRENCY STRENGTH

A is for ANALYSIS

E is for ENTRY

S is for STOP LOSS

E is for EXIT

R is for REPEAT THAT SHEET!!

2. Currency strength ...the foundation of my C.A.E.S.E.R method

3. Analysis: HOW CAN I LEARN to predict where THE FOREX MARKET will move next?

Currency pairs, relative currency strengths, trading strength versus weakness. How does currency strength give me an edge in Forex trading?

WHAT ARE THE FOREX BASICS? WHAT FORMS THE BREAD AND BUTTER?

Analysis: Support and Resistance....this is the essence.. buy lows, sell highs

that's all you need to know to have a profitable supper. Master these concepts and you will eat cake.

4. **ENTRY**. How do I get in and ENTER A TRADE Bulls, Bears, Trends?

5. **STOP LOSS**

6. **EXIT**

7. **REPEAT THAT SHEET**

The final countdown: WHAT CHECKLISTS DO I NEED FOR TRADING SPEED??

Mindset checklist

Risk management checklist

Broker setup checklist

Trading plan checklist: plan your trades and then trade your plan

References

Appendix: links to further education and key trading websites

Chapter 1

"Emancipate yourself from mental slavery, none but ourselves can free our minds." Bob Marley

What the Heck is Forex? ..and why should I read this book?? Forex is the biggest ocean of financial opportunity in the world. Five trillion dollars are traded in the forex market daily.

I repeat: **FIVE TRILLION DOLLARS ARE TRADED ON THE FOREX MARKET DAILY!!!**

When I started my Forex journey five years ago the market volume was 3 trillion dollars a day.

It is hard for most people to visualize a million or even a billion dollars. A trillion dollars is a thousand billion. I give you a detailed breakdown of what a trillion dollars looks like a little later.

Welcome to the world of Forex wealth.

Why are you here???? For each unique reader the answer will be a little different. I assume that all my readers are interested in wealth creation for a variety of reasons.

If you want to create or build wealth , then you are in the right place.

I have a companion book Fired Up Forex that will soon be available for advanced investors at www.firedupforex.com . Fired Up Forex provides more in-depth training on strategies for intermediate and advanced traders who wish to elevate their income and supersize their lives.

Why should you read this particular forex book??? What is it makes me unique ??

I have developed the ability to take complex investing concepts and teach them in a simple way that is easy for you to digest.

Forex life can be complicated.

It took tremendous effort for me to weed out the garden and lead you to exactly where the grass is greener.

I am a scientist, mathematician and a storyteller. This unique combination makes my book different from all the other Forex books that are often dry and analytical.

Investing and Forex training books tend to be difficult to read and even more difficult to understand.

Investing is an uncommon and very broad subject. Investing is mostly boring...but can be sexy if done right.

I am here to bring flavor so Forex tastes good. I want you to enjoy digesting these concepts; as I help you to make money.

Forex trading is making money trading money.

How exciting is that?? Who doesn't love making money??

Who am I and why should you listen to me??

I am a University of the West Indies trained physician. I have practiced medicine for a combined 20 years in Jamaica, Belize and now the U.S. (hence the Caribbean flavor)

I practice surgery daily in South Florida. I also have an undergraduate degree with honors in Biology and Mathematics from Regis University in Denver, CO.

My math and science background helped me to quickly understand some charting and trending concepts.

I am very good at spotting trends. I would like to show you what trends to look for when trading Forex.

Honestly, my stellar academic achievements were of very little use when I started Forex trading with my own real money.

Learning how to lose is the most important lesson in investing. When you lose...do not lose the lesson. The good thing is that any trader can and should determine how much the maximum loss will be BEFORE you enter the trade.

The STOP LOSS is the S of the six-step strategy I will outline.

You too will find anxiety when it is time to enter your first forex trades. Hundreds or thousands of your actual money may be lost.

Hundreds of thousands of dollars will be gained. A lot of your deeply hidden psychological demons will rear their ugly heads.

The most important thing in live forex trading is mastering your fears.

When we move beyond this phase we learn to control emotion. We must build a consistent wealth mindset to be consistently successful at forex specifically; and in life in general.

Once you remove emotions; then trading is just learning to plan your work and work your plan.

This book is all about getting you to the point of internal success, so you can manifest external success. I am here to direct you with a laser pointer to all the resources you need to get there.

Sign up for my free guidance of current forex tips and trends at www.firedupforex.com

Suggested plan: Practice trading a demo (dummy) account after you have read this book.

When you have done 100 trades you can start a small real account with $1000. With leverage this allows you to trade safely at 50cents per pip. 0.05 or half a mini-lot.

Net gain of 100 pips per trading day is the first goal.

That means trading wins minus losses adds $50 per day to your trading account.

That translates to consistent 5% growth every trading day.

That means that in ten days or two weeks of trading you it is possible to have $500 in profit when you started your account with $1000. You could do half as well and have $250 in profit.

There is a learning curve but it is important to trade your real money as this emotional journey is different than trading with play money.

What if it takes you four weeks or eight weeks to get to $500 profit. That is still a possible 50 percent profit in two months.

It is likely that most will take it up to one year to get to consistency.

Would it be worth it to have a skill that can generate 50% profit on any amount in one year? The appropriate answer is yes.

Keep in mind that once you master this skill it is possible to do the same thing in a day. I have personally witnessed one of my mentors generate $20,000 profit in one day.

I have personally interviewed an FX mentor who averages $50,000 net income per month trading a $200000 account. This was 5 years before I wrote this book.

Money deposited in bank savings accounts in the U.S.A. currently grow at 1-2% per year…if you are very lucky. Even a fixed deposit at a major bank yields 1.5% in 2018.

In learning forex trading we are looking at 1-2% net growth every trading day. Plus, there is no maximum. The nature of Forex is that there is no limit to how much you can grow.

Losing is terrible. *It is more important to learn how to lose than to learn how to win in Forex.*

Why do I say that? It is easy to continue trading if you are winning. If you lose 5 trades in a row then you must be sure that those losses did not wipe out your account (risk management)

I help to prepare you to trade. You must prepare your mind to absorb those losses psychologically.

You develop a winning mindset because you believe in the trading system and execute the trades according to the plan.

Success is a formula. By managing risk versus reward, you can be wrong on half of your trades and still take money to the bank. The top Forex traders in the world are only right on 6 to 7 out of every ten trades. (i.e. 60% of the time consistently)

Once you are consistently profitable and confident, you can start with $2000 or $5000 deposit in your broker account.

You can then trade $1 per pip or $5 per pip using the broker's leverage.

Net 100 pips per day means you are now gaining $100 to $500 net per trading day to your account. You will win some trades and you will lose some trades.

That is how trading works. You will be angry at yourself, your dog, your momma, and your broker when you lose.

If you are consistent and keep trading according to plan, you will eventually grow up and trade without emotion. That is when you approach mastery.

Master traders lose money. A master trader whose system I followed had net gains for 11 months. The month I joined his automated system, he lost for the first time.

There are no guarantees.

You can see that once you learn how to consistently gain pips, you can size up more profit in many ways.

You can take a bigger lot size

You can take more trades in the same currency

You can trade multiple currency pairs

You can lock in profit when the market moves in your direction for a risk free trade

EUR, GBP, AUD strong while USD, JPY, CHF weak

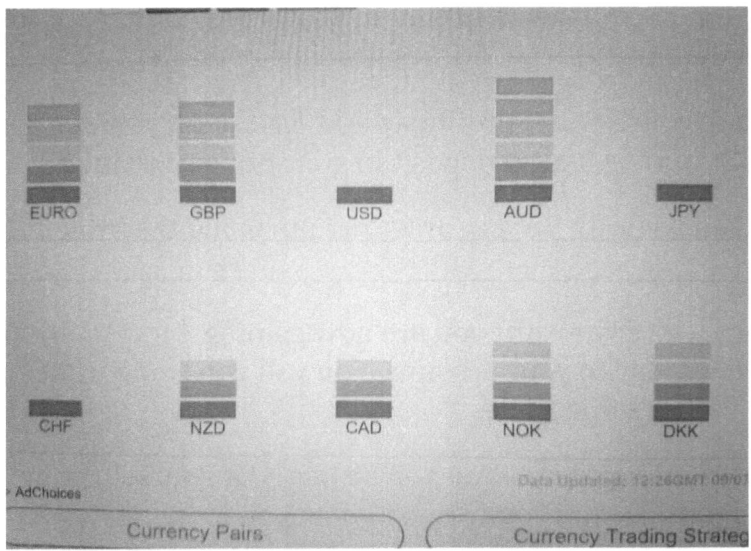

TRADING OPPORTUNITY ON MULTIPLE CURRENCY PAIRS

Why did I seek to learn and trade Forex???.

I have been an employed medical professional for the past 20 years. Though I enjoy helping and serving others, I have never enjoyed being an employee.

Employees may have a good income, but it is limited by the fact that someone else determines the maximum you are paid.

In America, you can be fired without cause at any time, and the laws are built to protect the corporations, not the individual.

Having an employer means there is always been a limit to what I can earn per hour.   I have worked an extra 12-hour Saturday night shift for a few years in the past.

This gave me $90,000 gross income. It also grossed me out.(American slang)

It also made me sick and tired all the time. Working 60 hours a week, 6 days a week; made me sick and tired of being sick and tired.

30% of my income as an employee automatically goes to the government in prepaid taxes. This disappears automatically without passing through my bank account. It is like earning monopoly money. Do not pass go.

Then another 20% went to recurrent bills and insurance payments.

Your situation may be similar to mine. As you read this you're your financial situation may much better or much worse .

The good news is this. It does not matter.

What matters is that if you learn to trade forex successfully, ***you determine your own income***. My close friend and mentor Mr. Paul Lecky often reminded me that **your income determines your outcome.**

Forex trading can help to put you on the road to where you want to be…regardless of where you are now.

The reality is that the high cost of living tends to outpace income even for highly paid employees.

My financial life in America has meant primarily being a slave to the clock and slave to an employer.

Most people that own a business may do better financially but are still limited by their business' demands on their time and freedom and income.

Anyone can trade Forex with a laptop and access to the internet. It takes focus and work, but this is true power.

It is the type of power that once you have it; no-one can take it away.

There are many millionaires and billionaires who fall into financial difficulty. The real powerful ones can earn it back quickly because of what they know.

There power is not in the money, it is in their knowledge.

I know Donald Trump may come to mind.. but many top investors have even more amazing stories...**believe me**!!

History
All symbols

Profit: 714.99
Balance: 714.99

AUDUSDi, buy 0.50 2017.07.11 06:08
0.76064 → 0.76148 **42.00**

USDCHFi, buy 0.50 2017.07.11 12:58
0.96682 → 0.96890 **107.34**

GBPCHFi, sell 0.50 2017.07.11 10:39
1.24389 → 1.24800 **-212.46**

EURNZDi, buy 0.50 2017.07.11 13:02
1.57053 → 1.57882 **299.15**

USDJPYi, buy 0.50 2017.07.11 13:02
114.091 → 114.321 **100.59**

GBPJPYi, buy 0.50 2017.07.11 13:02
146.932 → 147.570 **279.04**

EURJPYi, buy 0.50 2017.07.11 13:02
130.001 → 130.285 **124.20**

EURNZDi, buy 0.10 2017.07.11 10:30
1.57541 → 1.57579 **2.75**

The image above shows a screenshot of trading from a cell phone on the MT4 platform.

There are six pairs that are a buy and one pair that is a sell. 0.50 means that half a standard lot is being traded...or about $5 US per pip.

Just below each pair is shown the price the pair has moved since entry to the current market price

Hence, we entered a buy of AUD/USD at 0.76064 and the market has since moved up to price 0.76148

0.76148 - 0.76064 = .00084

8.4 pips movement at $5 a pip is approximately $40

Hence AUD/USD is showing $42 profit. GBP GBPJPY

killing it with $279 profit on this day trade!

Yes we can, forex traders...Yes we can!!

When I trade Forex, there is no limit on my income. When you learn to consistently profit trading Forex, there will be no limit to your income. This is what you have been looking for!!!!

Let that sink in. Learn to profit consistently trading Forex and there is no limit to your income.

There are many different paths to financial freedom. Forex is undoubtedly a path paved with gold, dollars, pound...and yen.

What the heck is Forex???? Now you know. Forex is essentially *pattern recognition for profit*. If you can do this well, unlimited profit is possible for you.

You can learn to earn independently for life.

I am grateful to be able to share what I have learnt about Forex with you.

Teaching has always helped me to become a better learner. I am helping you help me.

One key thing that investors overlook is the **_subconscious blocks to money that may have preset your wealth thermostat_**.

You may remain stuck financially regardless of what opportunity is presented.

Mindset matters matter.

It is critical to recognize that you have subconscious blocks that must be cleared before your mind allows you to embrace success.

The strategy is not your greatest challenge. I provide a simple strategy in this book.

This book is here to mentor you in your forex journey. Together we will work on identifying and mastering your mindset. Together we can focus on how to successfully navigate this ocean of Forex money without drowning in the process.

Come on baby!!

Let's get started.

Wait..... You need a life vest for safety first. If you intend to stay alive on your trading journey never trade without a <u>stop loss</u> (life vest).

What the heck is Forex???? I shall break Forex trading down so simply that even a baby can do it. Let's go....

Chapter 2.

WHAT THE HECK IS FOREX?

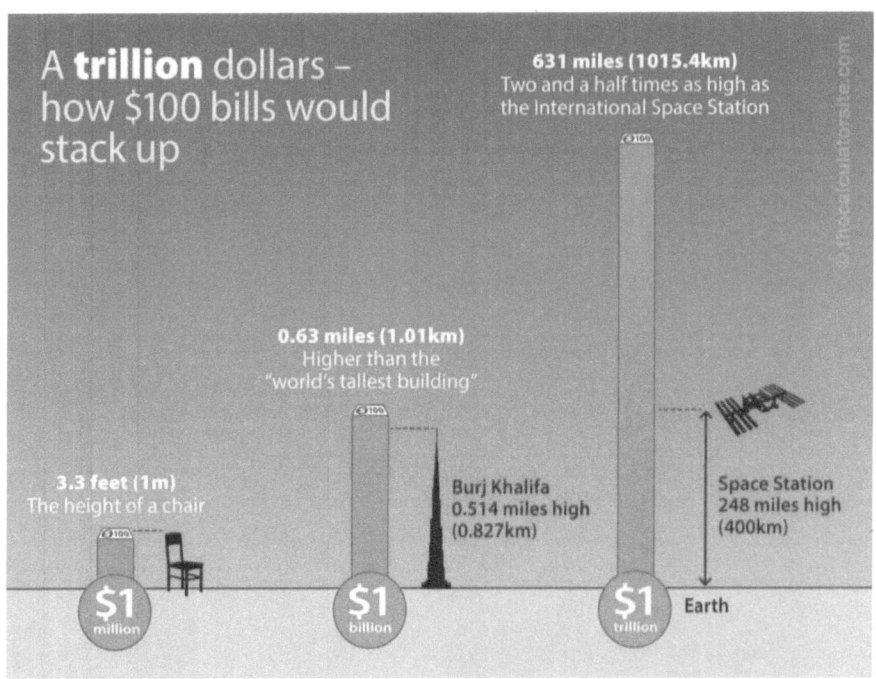

How much is a trillion dollars anyway?

$1000 is one thousand dollars

$1,000,000 is one million dollars

$1,000,000,000 is one billion dollars $1,000,000,000,000 is one trillion dollars

https://www.thecalculatorsite.com/articles/finance/howmuch-is-a-trillion.php

So, we now know that one trillion dollars has 12 zeros.

We are starting your journey from zero to hero... and that is a lot of zeros to accumulate. These figures may still mean very little to the average person who has never heard of Forex.

As a practical example: A stack of one trillion one-dollar bills lined up end to end would reach ¼ of the way to the moon and way ten tons or 20 000 pounds (weight not GBP)

My favorite explanation:

Imagine for a minute that you have one trillion-dollar bills ($1,000,000,000,000) stored in soccer stadium somewhere. You are told you need to spend it all.

You could **spend $54 million dollars every day of your life for 50 years and still have a few thousand in change left over.**

Those would be good times... Let us get ourselves in that forex wealth mindset.

Say to yourself: "Self: I have a trillion dollars to spend and not enough time to spend it."

That should make you feel great...make you feel like a trillion bucks....

That explains one trillion dollars.

Five trillion dollars value in currency is traded daily in the worldwide foreign exchange market. **WTF** ?book

WHAT THE HECK IS FOREX???

It is the biggest ocean of financial opportunity in the world.

I am going to give you highlights of this immense and complex market. There is a lot of information all over the internet universe once you start looking.

My intent is to give you an action-packed guide to the analysis and trading method that has empowered me in my trading.

I want you to memorize CAESER.

This old dude was one of the greatest thinkers and leaders of all time. He was the first to get his face on a coin (currency)

This is the mnemonic I created for you to rise from a disaster to a master of Forex.

The letters are my method to focus your attention on what is important to trade.

This is how we do it!   We awaken the riches of your inner Emperor.

CAESAR

I know CAESER is not the correct spelling of the great emperor's name, but it is my exercise of poetic license.

I want you to master Forex wealth even if you lose the spelling bee and fail at spelling. You will be so rich it will not matter.

Your mental image of your inner champion is what really matters.

You want to be a Forex baller and a shot caller. I hope you get the point, currency kings and queens.

We are here to awaken your inner emperor...or empress.

C   CURRENCY Currency strength measure. Start here by determining which currency pair or pairs are most suitable to trade. Are you looking to buy or sell?

A   ANALYZE Analyze the chart quicker and better. Once you have decided, go to the live market chart of that currency. Apply analysis to find an optimum entry.

E   ENTRY Enter trade direction. Buy a low of support or sell a high of resistance. Look for past levels of support or resistance that have created pivot point levels.

S   STOP Stop loss protection. You set this when you enter the trade as you determine how much of your account you will lose if the trade does not go as you predicted. Risk vs. reward

E   EXIT Exit determines your profit. It is best to have a fixed exit for all trades as a beginning trader. You want to know where you are getting out of the trade. Profit is made on the exit.

R   REPEAT that sheet sh$#t. Cursing helps memory... trust me. How committed are you to your Forex success??? Repeat that sheet. Repeat that sheet.

Repetition is the key to consistent success. Practice. Practice . Practice. This is all about pattern recognition for profit.

You want to ingrain winning habits. It is critical to repeat this exact same process for 100 trades. Practice this rhyme to win with time

Here is a **CAESER** rhyme if rapping is your pleasure:

CURRENCY strength measure

ANALYZE charts better

ENTER trade in the right direction

STOP your loss for protection

EXIT for profit

REPEAT that sheet (sh#$t)

Seize your inner Caesar. Do not panic or have a seizure.

Everyone can tap into their inner greatness ,

Practice, practice, practice; and eventually master forex.

I have to check if Jay-Z may be interested in these lyrics.

You never know until you ask....

Back to the lesson at hand.

Break down your wealth blocks and rebuild your wealth mindset. You cannot earn more than you have learned. You can only be as wealthy as your dominant thoughts allow you to be. The actual technical concepts of forex are simple to master with study and practice.

Mindset mastery is the hardest part of your forex journey to success.

Set a vision and a goal. If you do not have a target how do you know if you are making progress?

1. <u>Set and define a goal</u> that you wish to become a successful Forex trader. We start with the knowledge that only 20% of Forex traders are consistently successful long term. You must define what success means to you. Your why must be strong enough to make you cry. Define your why and write it down.
2. <u>Educate yourself</u>. I am glad you are here. This book is a comprehensive start on your journey. Read on.
3. <u>Learn how the market moves</u>
4. <u>Understand support and resistance</u>
5. <u>Define your edge</u>. I focus on currency strength versus weakness to predict where the market will move next. There are many ways of analysis in forex, but my focus is to teach you how to interpret FX direction and trade in that direction using currency strength indicators as your edge.
6. Choose a reputable broker and <u>open a demo (practice) account.</u> Practice. Practice. Practice. When you have analyzed executed a thousand trades you will be much better than after the first 100. The only way to get there is to follow the steps and just do it. C.A.E.S.E.R.
7. Understand <u>risk versus reward</u> and <u>practice</u> it on every trade. Risk only 1-2% of your total account balance with each trade you enter. Your stop loss is your life jacket.
8. Open a real account with at least US $1000. Risk 1% per trade means that you can safely trade about $0.50 per pip using leverage. One goal as beginners is to net 50 pips per day. That is net $25 per day to your $1000 account. 20 profitable trading days(one month of trading) nets $25 X20=$500.

The time taken to get there will be different for each individual trader but worth it for all traders who stick to the plan.

9. Practice trading CAESER. The idea is to build a consistent skill. Stay inspired by the knowledge a profit of $6000 net trading over ten months to a year is possible, even for a beginner starting with $1000. It has been done many times before in less time.
10. Intermediate traders can access advanced forex trading strategies and mentorship to profit faster at www.firedupforex.com

Chapter 3
HOW DOES THE FOREX MARKET MOVE?

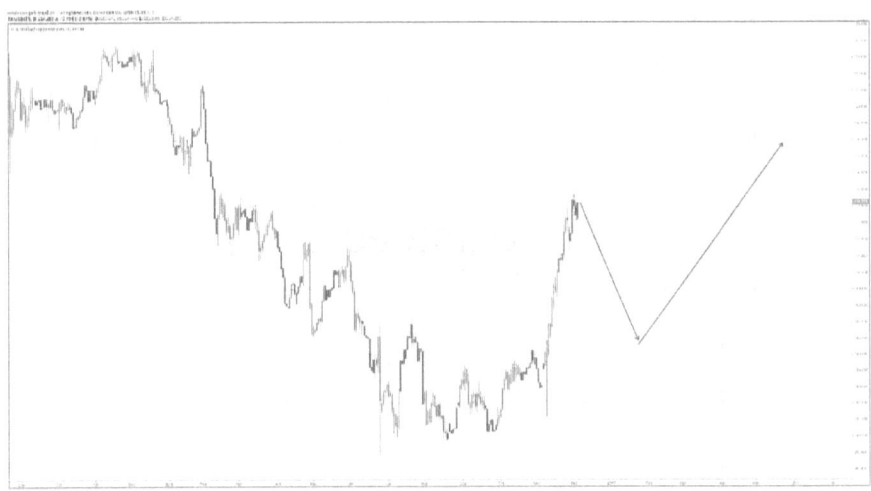

The forex market moves either up (bullish), down (bearish) or sideways (consolidation). A successful trader needs to have an edge in analyzing the market.

As a top trader, we must believe that your insight into the market can correctly predict whether the market is going up, down or sideways.

We must be profitable 7 out of every 10 times that we enter a trade to have great success.

Consistent profit is not only picking the right direction. With proper risk reward ratio, we can be right only half the time and still make a net profit on our trades.

Currency strength trading is the edge that I believe in. I did not find success until I learned in depth currency strength analysis from hedge fund manager James at Complete Currency Trader.

He provides a free online currency strength indicator and terrific beginner and advanced training.

The currencies in the forex market are bought and sold in pairs. Currency traders seek out strong currencies and buy them. Traders seek out weak currencies and sell them.

Out of the 28 main currency pairs that are bought and sold on any trading day, the charts that are moving the most are the pairs in which one currency is getting weaker and the other is getting stronger. This is the edge: pair strong with weak.

Let us look at the GBP/USD pair. Not all pairs are created equal and this is the most commonly traded pair. The USD is the gold standard of forex.

60% of all trades occur during the London financial market. A large percentage of all trades are GBP/USD.

Great British Pound GBP is the dominant currency of this pair.

The dominant currency is listed first in any currency pair.

- A. Any economic event or announcement that strengthens the Great British Pound will cause GBP/USD chart to move up (bullish)
- B. Any economic event or announcement that weakens the Great British Pound will cause GBP/USD chart to move down (bearish)

The USD also affects the movement on this pair.

- C. Any economic event or announcement that strengthens the USD will cause GBP/USD chart to move down (bearish)
- D. Any economic event or announcement that weakens the USD will cause the GBP/USD chart to move up (bullish) This is the essence of currency strength analysis .

It allows traders to look at the relative strength of individual currencies within the pairs to determine direction.

Profit in forex lies in picking the right direction of market movement and then trading in that direction.

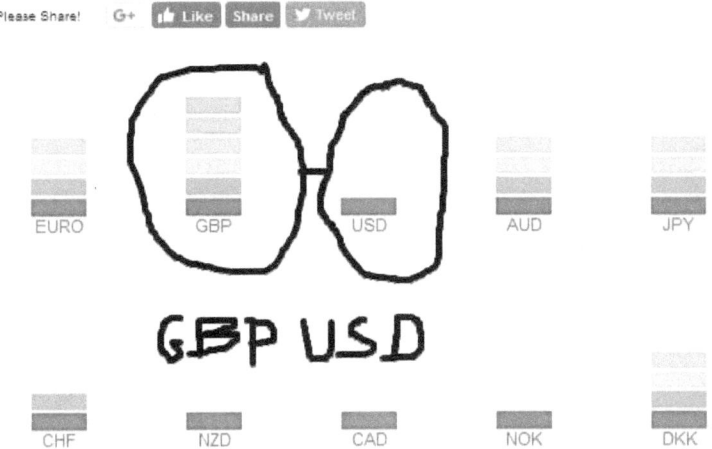

The biggest movement upward (bullish) on the GBP/USD occurs when GBP is strengthening at the same time USD is weakening. (This means buy GBP/USD for big profit)

Most traders see the trend and start jumping in as buyers. This leads to less GBP availability (more demand) and quick increase in price of the pair. Bullish trend.

The opposite holds true:

The biggest movement downward (bearish) on the GBP/USD occurs when GBP is weakening at the same time USD is strengthening. (This means sell GBP/USD for big profit)

The majority of traders will see the trend and start jumping in as sellers of this currency pair.

This leads to more GBP availability (more supply) and quick decrease in the price of the pair. Bearish trend.

Measuring Currency Strength and Weakness

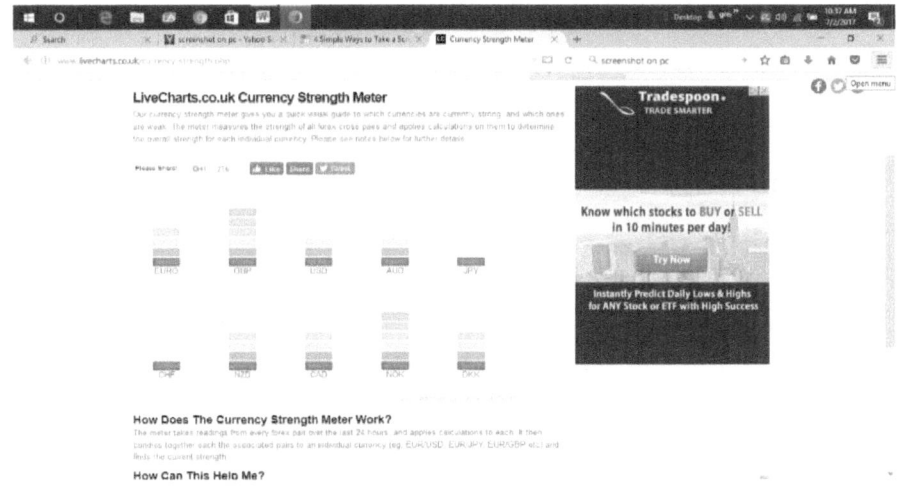

This image shows live charts free currency strength meter. www.livecharts.co.uk/currency-strength.php

It shows the relative strengths of the main currencies.

This is where I go to quickly scan the live forex market. I then look at which currency pair may be ideal to trade at any given time.

I perform analysis on that pair and decide if I should enter a trade.

How does it work? This screenshot shows that GBP is very strong

It also shows that CHF (Swiss franc) and JPY (Japanese yen)are very weak.

That usually means traders will want to buy the pound and sell the yen.

1. The GBP/JPY pair is being actively traded.
2. Traders are bullish on GBP/JPY
3. Look for buying opportunity on GBP/JPY.

4. CHF or Swiss franc is also very weak. Look to enter a buy trade on GBP/CHF as well.
5. Plan your trade and trade your plan.
6. Stick to the plan, use your currency strength analysis edge, apply risk management to entry and exit, and profit consistently.

Once you understand how to analyze and trade GBP/JPY. You can apply the same concepts to analyze and trade any of the 28 main currency pairs.

The 2 charts below show how currency strength analysis can reveal trading opportunity on the AUD/CHF.

This is a clear example of how **understanding patterns in Forex can translate into profits.**

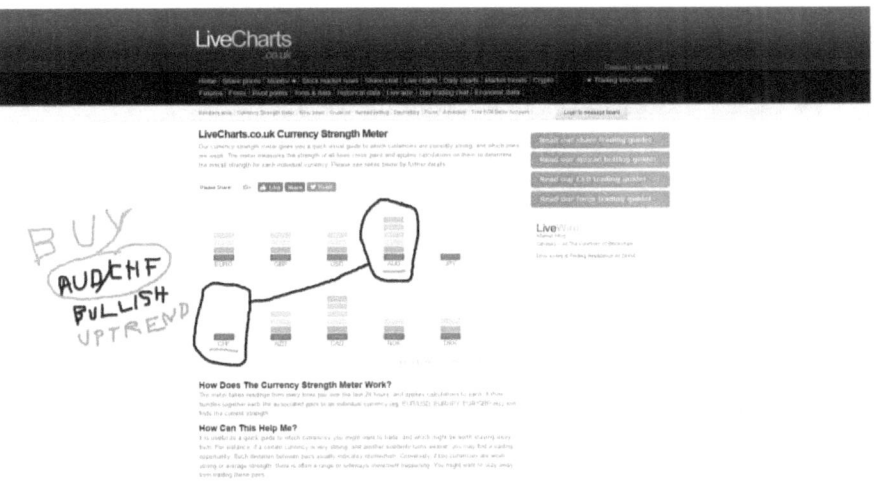

AUD is strong, and CHF is weak on the currency strength meter. We pair strongest with weakest and we look at the AUDCHF chart for opportunity.

The second image shows the AUDCHF hourly chart. Buying in the past 20 hours would have netted 100 pips or more.

Great profit for one day of trading. That is just one of many currency pairs available to trade.

Chapter 4

WHAT ARE THE FOREX BASICS?? WHAT ARE THE BREAD AND BUTTER OF CURRENCY TRADING?

Bulls, bears, Support and Resistance...that's all you need to know to have a profitable supper. Master these concepts and you will eat cake (profit).

Currency pairs make up the charts that are traded in the forex market. These pairs are constantly moving in waves. The charts move up, down and sideways.

Dr. Vinoop says a chart is a chart is a chart. You can analyze and trade commodities like gold, oil and silver in a similar way to GBP/USD.

This mentor is a position trader who analyzes primarily support and resistance, regardless of what he is trading.

The market will either move up, down or sideways (consolidate or range).

Forex is unique in that you can enter the market at any time as a buyer or as a seller of currency.

When you enter a trade, you must decide if you are a bull or a bear.

Apart from the fact that they are obviously different animals, these terms have special meanings in financial markets.

I like the graphic image of being under attack by either animal. It helped me to visualize the difference.

What is a Bull?

<u>**A bull**</u> attacks and tosses you upwards. Bull traders think the market is going up and enter a trade buying (long).

If I am bullish GBP I will buy GBP/USD and other GBP pairs. If I am bullish on gold I will buy gold. If I am bullish on Amazon I will buy Amazon stock.

Bulls are buyers who push the market up. Bulls see strength or believe the market is strengthening.

If you believe Australia is doing well economically or politically, you will want to buy currency pairs AUD/USD and AUD/JPY.

You decide to enter the market buying

    a. Buy for a few minutes and close the trade.. you are a Scalper

b. Buy for a few hours and close the trade... you are a day trader.
c. Buy for a few weeks or months and then close the trade. You are a position (long term) trader.

What is a bear?

A bear attacks and beats you downward. Picture a huge grizzly bear approaching you on hind legs.

Bear Traders think the market is going **down** and **enter selling (short)**. If I am **bearish** Canadian dollar (CAD), I will sell CAD/JPY and other CAD pairs.

If I am bearish on silver I will sell silver. If I am bearish on cheeseburgers I may sell McDonalds stock.

Bears are sellers who think the markets are weakening and it is time to sell or (short) the currency.

If you are bearish on the UK economy or politics then you will sell the GBP (aka the pound). (Brexit is coming....fear the bears)

You therefore decide to enter the market selling

a. Sell for a few minutes and close the trade.. you are a Scalper

b. Sell for a few hours and close the trade... you are a day trader.

c. Sell for a few weeks or months and then close the trade. You are a position (long term) trader.

In Forex trading, the time frame determines what type of trader you are. It is important to determine what time frame fits your personality type.

Q: Will hourly, daily or weekly trades bring you passion and profit long term?

Do you want to make quick profits and quick losses and get out? Then scalping may be your thing.

Do you want to trade for a few hours every trading day and hold a position for one or two nights the most? Then you are a day trader.

Do you want to enter a long-term trade, set it and forget it for a month or six months? Then you are a position trader.

This is how Dr V rolls...and he is rolling in dollars. Successful position traders amass huge wealth. They hold positions for months until the price reaches the target.

The market moves hundreds and thousands of pips profit in each trade over those months.

Each type of trading has its advantages and disadvantages.

You can decide what style or combination of trading styles works best for you.

Personally, I find day trading and long-term trading less stressful. This more in tune with how I like to trade.

I have chronic high blood pressure and scalping is like a pressure cooker for me. The stress does not do well for my state of mind nor my bank account.

It may work for you. A pressure cooker produces rapid meals in very short amounts of time. On the other hand, if you do not know how to use it safely; the results could be disastrous

On a side note, you can check out my Belize Cookbook at A http://www.amazon.com/dp/B00H1CVSMY
The fact I love to cook almost as much as I love to eat. I am a bestselling cookbook author. This is for those of you who wish to explore and enjoy some exotic Caribbean cuisine.

We are exploring deep fundamental concepts critical to your trading success. It is important to relax and let these ideas *simmer*... (I hope you see what I did there..)

Chapter 5
SUPPORT AND RESISTANCE

Floor of support and Ceiling of resistance

Dr Vinoop is an anesthesiologist who is a good friend and my favorite mentor. He is a leader on our surgical team and we have practiced medicine together for the past seven years.

He has also mentored me on trading. He is a self-taught and very successful trader. There seems to be no limit to his knowledge, wisdom and humility.

Dr. V is a position trader. I have missed out on thousands of dollars of opportunity many times when I don't listen to where he tells me the FX markets are headed in a few months.

He trades using primarily support and resistance to analyze the market long term.

Dr V applies the principles of SUPPORT and RESISTANCE equally to analyze and trade stocks, commodities and currencies.

There are thousands of different forex indicators and systems to predict market movement.

Most of them measure hidden levels of support and resistance.

I am addressing these concepts as they are literally the bread and butter of basic trading.

SUPPORT is a FLOOR

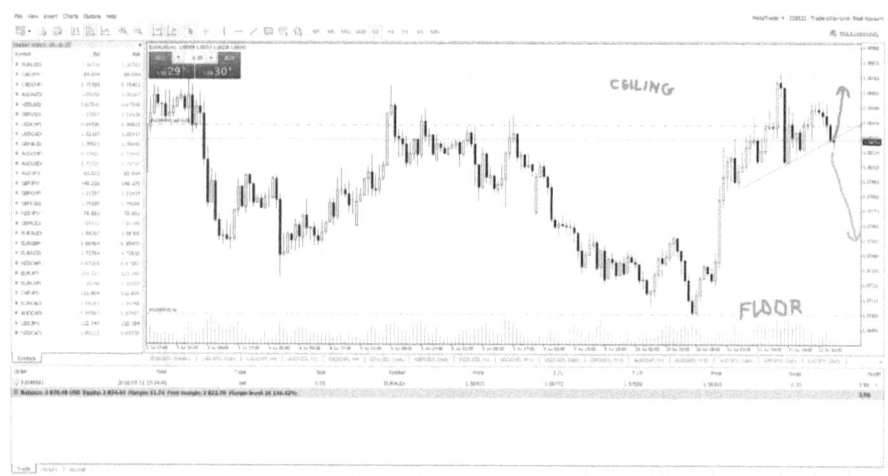

Buyers or bulls provide support. When a market direction is downward it is being dominated by sellers (bears). More people are shorting the currency pair than are buying.

At some point the buyers step in and start buying in large numbers. The selling spree comes to an end and the buyers take over (supporting the currency).

This level of change from seller to buyer dominance forms turning point (pivot) on the chart (low)

RESISTANCE is a CEILING

Sellers or bears provide resistance. When market direction is upward it is being dominated by buyers (bulls).

More traders are buying the currency pair than are selling. At some future point the sellers step in and start selling in large numbers.

The buying spree comes to an end and the sellers take over

(provide a ceiling of resistance)

This level of change from buyer to seller dominance forms a turning point (pivot) on the chart (high)

As a general principle, past levels of support and resistance tend to become future levels of support and resistance.

Why is this true??

Traders tend to enter and exit the market buying or selling at levels where large amounts of buyers or sellers entered or exited in the past.

On any chart, look left. Past movement is one of the best predictors of future movements. Study the upcoming chart on pivot points well until you grasp this important concept.

Now, you have decided it is time to buy.

The next step is to determine when is the best time to ENTER a trade buying.

You want to look for the next level of support. It is a signal that buyers are taking over or dominating the market.

This also applies if you want to sell (short) the market.

You want to determine when is the best time to ENTER the market selling. You want to predict the next level of resistance. Look for a signal that sellers are taking over and dominating the market.

Pivot Points (strong levels of Support and Resistance)

The diagram above shows a **pivot point line**(thick red line) on a daily chart.

This means that each candlestick consists of the range of price movement on the currency pair over 24 hours.

The whole chart shows how price has moved over the course of a few months to a year.

The thick red line is a price pivot point for this currency.

Notice how the currency chart tends to pivot (U-turn) whenever it approaches this price point (Red Line)

Traders look at patterns. Of high interest are:

    a. **Levels of support** – blue circles at the floor of support
    b. **Levels of resistance** – blue circles at the ceiling of resistance
    c. **Past support becoming future resistance** – the first small blue circle in the big red pivot point line shows a floor support.

       The other 3 small blue circles show it becoming resistance at a future time

d. **Past resistance becoming future support**

e. **Pivot point level** Big red line shows a major pivot point price level for this currency pair. It does not even matter which currency pair this is. All pairs behave in a similar fashion and follow these principles.

Traders eagerly try to predict pivot points to determine when to:

1. ENTER the market buying or selling
2. EXIT the market buying or selling if already in a trade
3. STAY OUT of the market if the trade setup does not fit the plan

STAYING OUT of a choppy market is often more important to consistent long-term profits than entering a trade.

This point cannot be emphasized enough. All the times when I have tried to chase a market trend and jumped in the market half-heartedly has resulted in my losing money on the trade.

Please understand that when you apply currency strength analysis you will start to see a lot of missed opportunity and want to jump in to catch the end of the move.

The market will reverse direction and stop you out almost as soon as you do this. No Bueno.

It is human nature to let our greed exceed our need.

This is where discipline and managing our own emotions is key.

It is even more critical to our consistent success than applying a technical strategy to the markets.

Which Forex mentor is right for you?

There are many forex mentors that get caught up in teaching students to analyze the market and forget to focus on teaching the steps of actual trading.

When I first learnt forex trading, I became entranced by the mathematical precision of how the market can move to fulfill a Fibonacci mathematical sequence.

I have not used Fibonacci's in the three years since I was taught currency strength analysis and it worked well for me.

It is important that you determine what type of trader you are and follow those mentors who will teach you to trade based on your individual strengths.

If you master yourself and have a strong foundation; you can be successful with any system.

If you attempt to trade someone else's method or system without understanding the fundamentals..you are doomed to failure....or bankruptcy as you try to figure it out.

My first mentors were very good at communicating theory.

In practice, I felt lost when I tried to apply their theories to trade my account.

I don't want this to happen to you. That is the reason I take an oversimplified introductory approach.

The shortcut you really need to master are the steps of CAESER..

C

HOW DO I DETERMINE CURRENCY STRENGTH

A

HOW DO I READ CHARTS TO CONFIRM A BULLISH OR BEARISH TREND ON MY CURRENCY PAIR OF CHOICE

E

WHERE DO I GET IN? HOW EXACTLY DO I ENTER A TRADE?

S

WHERE DO I PUT MY STOP LOSS?? HOW MANY PIPS CAN I LOSE IF THE MARKET MOVES AGAINST MY ANALYZED TRADING DIRECTION?

E

WHERE DO I GET OUT TO MAXIMIZE MY CHANCE OF PROFIT??

R

RINSE AND REPEAT...THE IMPORTANCE OF PRACTICE

We already looked at currency strength and weakness analysis via the livecharts meter.

Complete currency trader James Edward has an in depth teaching on this.

He also has a free meter available on his website. His currency strength meter is dynamic.

It can help you to analyze trends in currency strength over the past minutes, hours and days.

He does provide excellent free introductory training in his webinar.

I explore how to use his free currency meter to advance trade in my upcoming book : **Fired Up Forex**

Most of the other questions can be answered by the market movement and turning points.

We explored highs and lows, support and resistance, and pivot points

Identifying these patterns form the ideal entry and exit points for all types of trading.

In Forex we have an almost limitless opportunity for profit. We can enter the market at any time as either a buyer or a seller.

The universal investment advice still holds true.

We want to buy low and sell high.

Traders want to **buy a low at a level of support** and **sell a high at a level of resistance**.

We want to predict where the next turning point of the market will most likely be.

Why??

The currency markets are constantly moving, up, down and sideways.

The most useful indicators are ones that show us where the market is turning (pivot points).

It is easy to spot a bullish market. The chart is waving upward as price action of the currency pair gets higher and higher.

It is easy to spot a bearish market. The chart is waving downwards, and price action gets lower and lower.

What may be difficult to predict consistently is where the market will turn.

Where will the bullish move become bearish?

Where will the bearish move become bullish?

Let us imagine you are already in a trade.

You are a bull and have entered the market buying at a low of support (turning point). The market waves upward.

You want to get out for profit the next time the market turns downward.

To profit as a buyer you must exit the market at a price above where you got in.

If you exit at the same level you entered, you break even.

If you exit at a price lower than you entered you lose money.

We need to know where to get out for profit. Where is the EXIT??

The next turning point of the currency pair you are trading may be at a past level of market support.

It may occur at a past level of market resistance.

It may occur at a pivot point.

You may get a warning when you recognize a strong bearish candlestick formation happening.

If the bears are taking over it may be time to abandon the buy trade and get ready to sell.

That is why all these concepts are important. Understanding these protect your profit and prevent loss when you are trading.

Summary of Forex trading method and your opportunity

Forex is unique in that you can also enter the market as a seller. We profit by buying low and selling high like the stock market.

However, in forex we can enter by selling a high of resistance (turning point) and then exit by buying a low of support (turning point).

It is just the opposite of entering as a buyer described above.

This can be confusing. I do not want you to get confused. Just know that as a forex trader you can make money buying in the right direction

You can also make money selling in the right direction.

You can be a buyer and seller in the forex market many times in the same trading day...even within the same hour.

You can sell GBP/USD when the London market opens at 3 am Eastern.

When the US market opens at 8am Eastern ,the market may turn as US traders and events start to impact the USD.

You may decide to exit your sell trade and buy this same pair as the traders become bullish GBP/USD. You are now a buyer.

Later in the evening the market may turn again, and you may decide to sell the pair. You enter a sell order and you are once again a seller.

If you correctly assess the direction the market is moving at the precise time you trade, you can profit.

You ENTER buying while the market is moving up.

You can also EXIT when it turns back downward.

You then have the option to ENTER selling when the market starts moving downward.

The following images show bearish movement generating profit after a sell order.

BEFORE SELL ORDER

AFTER SELL ORDER

WHY DOES MY WEALTH MINDSET MATTER??

We saved the most difficult challenge for last...the trader's mindset and emotional intelligence.

How do I recognize and release my psychological and emotional blocks to creating, keeping and growing wealth and success?

My buddy Barry Baroudi catches and releases tarpon and is one of the best fishermen in Florida.

Before you can release...you have to be able to catch.

We cannot release mental blocks that we do not know we have.

This applies to Forex trading, but to everything else in your life. Mindset is the most important matter.

I personally would exit trades early because of fear of loss.

I come from humble beginnings and my mind kept telling me to cut and run once my trade was in profit.

I had to recognize this as a weakness and keep my hands off my trade and stick to the plan.

Fx chief taught us not to fiddle with a trade once executed. But I would be driven by forces only my inner child could comprehend!

You must face your own demons of fear and greed on your trading journey. You can triumph , yes you can!!

Forex trading is an incredible, incomparable tool to build wealth. It is a tool. The success or failure of your forex journey is subject to user error. The reality is that only 10-15 percent of those who attempt to trade Forex profit consistently.

Why do so many who attempt Fx trading fail?

- They do not have enough education. If you are here reading this book you are being educated - do not have a trading plan

- do not believe in their edge or skill

- destroy their account due to poor risk management

- do not believe in their potential for success at trading or anything they attempt for positive change

- are dominated by fear and greed

- have deep hidden psychological blocks to money, profits, and financial success

Thoughts lead to Feelings

Feelings lead to Actions

Actions create our Reality

T Harv Eker .   hence. Our thoughts become our reality ..

Every success and failure in our lives today is determined by our dominant and subconscious thoughts and beliefs.

Neville Goddard ...our thoughts become things

Why haven't you created financial abundance yet??? I have outlined a system that you can follow to success. If you are like me you have seen, learned and invested in many wealth building systems in the past.

Perhaps we need to look deeper at your beliefs. What do you believe???

Do you believe

- nothing good comes easily

- rich people are bad

- Money is evil

- money does not grow on trees

- you always end up spending more than you earn

- you cannot make money in this economy

- the banks and the government are out to get you and keep you broke

If you have these and other negative financial beliefs then somehow you will make bad trading decisions and end up losing the money you make trading

Your mindset will trump skill every time in the long run.

Success is an inside job.

Work on your financial, money blueprint and then you will manifest the success you see in the master traders.

Because everything looks easy when the master traders do it, does not mean it will be easy for you.

I am here to reveal possibility and potential of this immense financial market. I am not here to provide any guarantees to your success.

Success had a U (You) in it. "You" U is the most important letter in SUCCESS.

It commonly takes ten years or more to make an overnight success.

If you are seeking a quick fix, then beware. You may easily drown . The fact is that up to 85% of traders who attempt to swim in the Forex ocean drown.

They sink their account before they can learn how to consistently earn

Just because there is a trillion-dollar ocean of money does not mean that the majority don't drown in it.

I want you to be successful. That is why I wrote this book.

I want to make a positive difference in your life so that you can make a difference in the lives of others that depend on you.

That is why I am grateful to you for giving me the opportunity to be able to guide and help you.

I elevate my own knowledge and skills by packaging what I have learnt and teaching it to you.

I invite you to follow my entertaining and educational videos on YouTube.

Subscribe so that you can ask questions and share your challenges in your trading journey. I am developing a training course to serve you and your specific questions are important.

You are welcome to follow me on my Facebook page (FiredupForex) and sign up for my fired up forex email newsletter www.firedupforex.com

You can receive weekly emails and continued Forex mentorship and support daily from my unique perspective.

I am almost finished writing a book of advanced forex strategies that will be available to my list at www.firedupforex.com.

Thank you, gracias, merci , grazie

Thank you for purchasing this book. Thank you for taking action.... Most people do not even take one small step toward their dreams.

I am hopeful that you can answer confidently the next time someone asks you what the heck is forex?

You should also be able to use this book as a guide on your own journey to consistent wealth building by trading the Forex market.

Please utilize the website links I have provided at the end for further education and assistance with your journey.

Signature

Gregory Arana

Author

For More Information ,Suggestion & Feedback Please write an Email: gregory.arana@gmail.com

CURRENCY STRENGTH METER AT

www.livecharts.co.uk/currency-strength.php

ANNOUNCEMENTS AFFECTING THE CURRENCY MARKETS

www.forexfactory.com FOREX

CHARTS

www.tradingview.com

REPUTABLE BROKER FOR US TRADERS www.forex.com

INTERNATIONAL FOREX BROKER WITH GOOD LEVERAGE www.tradersway.com

SEARCHABLE ALL AROUND GREAT INVESTMENT KNOWLEDGE

www.investopedia.com

www.ingramcontent.com/pod-product-compliance
Lightning Source LLC
Chambersburg PA
CBHW021510210526
45463CB00002B/969